TIME-BOUND

TIME-BOUND

poems by

Kurt Brown

Tiger Bark Press • Rochester, NY • 2012

Published by Tiger Bark Press,
202 Mildorf Ave., Rochester, NY 14609.

Design by Philip Memmer.

ISBN-13: 978-0-9816752-7-5
ISBN-10: 0-9816752-7-1

What an outrage! This very moment gone forever.

—*Charles Simic*

CONTENTS

Acknowledgements

About the Author

I

THAT STREET

That street lined with poplars, elms and oaks,
shadow-webbed, star-ceilinged, wind-trafficked
by blowing snow—is it still there, its shimmering
pavements and empty lots, its hedged-in back
yards with their plastic pools, their toy balls
scattered near one-car paint-flaking garages?

And the sad, brown houses sinking into earth
with their many-peaked sun-crowned roofs,
windows from which tears and laughter,
bits of screams drifted out into slow moving dusks—
are they standing with their grim chimneys,
their coal bins and wide stoops like stone tongues?

And what about the lawns, squares of sparse grass
edging up through sand, acorn-drummed,
squirrel-haunted lawns where a boy's bicycle
lay abandoned, guarded by somnolent dogs
who barked their displeasure at each lone walker
whistling for night to come, come lie at his feet?

You can walk down that same street, right now,
but it's not that street. It still exists, but do you?
Even now it is within reach, there across the river,
though this sentence will never find it, these words
that wander blindly in their meanings looking
for its leaf-lined adjectives, its lost nouns of light.

PRESENT TENSE

The trick, say gurus, is to *stay in the present*
though even while saying it, the present flees.

Words disappear into past-time by the end
of the sentence which proposes to arrest it.

Time is money, we say, but it is also language.
Words take time and split it into separate realms.

The present seems the thinnest membrane
between past and future, the sliver of an instant

we pass through without ever being there.
Before, we say, and *after* and *now.*

But isn't that what childhood is all about,
a pre-verbal idyll without time

before the snake of language slithered in and hissed
you are dying, you will die, you have died.

PRACTICE

Lung-sore in summer heat
we scrambled up a bank
to steel our legs while Coach yelled
Go! Go! and sweat pebbled
our brows. The bank
rose steeply rank with sumac
from a field behind our school
and we strove up sucking wind
with every step, four-abreast,
then broke into pairs at the top—
two left, two right—and straggled down
again to get in line for more.
It was only August, but our team
held practice every weekend
to shape us up before the season
started. Adolescence
was an uphill grind, bodies
growing stronger and alert to possibilities
we'd only dreamed of,
watching heroes duke it out
on drive-in screens, then carry
the ladies off in their arms.
No pain, no gain! Coach roared,
so up we labored, dull-eyed Sisyphuses,
hearts hammering, heads packed
with big ideas. But all the while
the future waited with its certain failures,
its disappointments and defeats,
no matter how hard we worked,
how much we sweated
towards the top to stumble
down again, red-faced, aglow,
undaunted in the burning afternoon,
full of ambition to *Go! Go!*

THE CATCH

The home team spreads itself
into a busy diamond of quick boys
Coach hectors in a booming voice:
Jimmy, come on in; Mike, wake up, now!
And Davis, back up in case it's long!
Chatter leaps among them, hurling taunts
as a batter steps into the box
and paws the dirt. The first pitch
floats down the pike, and the batter
steps forward to send it out to right
where Davis waits almost casually,
not moving from his spot
until the ball begins to curve
downward in its flight. We hold our breath
as Davis rises on one leg and thrusts
his glove into the air to snatch it
in one clean swipe, the way a trout
drifts upward to seize a fly. Such a mundane
moment never quite disappears
but keeps recurring in a hundred guises
as it flutters back down to us through the years.

HARLOW

Hair hot-ironed to a waffled platinum,
corrugated mane that gave off light,
half girl-of-our-dreams, half
harlot, plump and khol-eyed
as an Egyptian queen. She out-vamped Dietrich,
and didn't care for niceties, screen
sophisticates gussied-up for a ball.
Most divas lounged in luxury, heavy
lidded sirens smoldering in style.
Even Garbo was a sylph with a patrician air.
She beat them all, our beautiful frump
who could snarl like a gangster's moll,
an American twang we loved
that cut the crap and got directly to the point:
"I like to wake up each morning
feeling a new man." In certain lights
her face looked bruised, almost
lumpy, an aging boxer's boozed-up mug.
Slapped, she shot back "Do it again,
I like it!" And we liked it too,
all that spunk confronting a muscled goon.
Lizard-sleek in gold lamé, she slunk
across the set to pout, a petulance
made famous for the way she picked
at bon bons while the nation starved.
At twenty six she died on cue, first
of the bombshell beauties, as though her sassiness
were toxic and her sins unexcused.
But those sins were virtues to us,
a bunch of horny Adams ripe for a fall.
Her exit line? From *Red Headed Woman:*
"I don't need a guide," she sneered.
"And don't call me madame."

ABOUT TIME

Real time, prime time, quality time, face time—
aren't we just talking about life but parsing it
into separate orders of experience? But experience
of what: attention, existence, consciousness?

Isn't time like the wind—everywhere an agent,
but invisible, blowing leaves, knocking down houses,
shoving the sea from one continent to the next?

Time itself is a destroyer. But it's also a Creator.
Sounds crazy, but that's the real enigma of Time.

And where does time abide, where does it live:
in cuckoo clocks (19th century time), or wristwatches
(20th century time), or sundials (14th century time)?
And if time moves one way, why not another?
Can we travel back on it, as Speke and Burton
traveled up the Nile to reach its ultimate source?

Time funnels through an hour glass, though
it's only sand squeezing through a pinched spot,
and sand isn't time, though it takes ages to make,
the grist of innumerable ground rocks.
                                        Arguments
about Time tend to end this way—where they began.
Yet time is everything, even though it's nothing.

Though not for us. For us it is everything, my love.

AT THE SUMMER LAKE CLUB

He'd come in every weekday afternoon
to play the organ, a battered Hammond
he acquired years ago, like his repertoire—
standards, mostly, "Ebb Tide" and "Caravan,"
songs as out-of-date as the double-breasted
suits he'd wear, thin and thready at the seams.
He was Charlie, our weekday entertainment,
though Saturdays, when diners filled the room,
a modern trio pumped out cloying pop,
and Sunday brunch was piped-in classical—
Hindemith and Mozart, strains of Schubert
for a crowd decked-out in their Sabbath best.
I was the bartender that year, eager
to learn my trade and keep the patrons happy,
just a kid adrift until that fall when
grad school beckoned and I'd give up slinging
drinks for Tennyson and Shakespeare.
Charlie would arrive and order a scotch:
"First things first," he'd say, then narrow his eyes
with pleasure as he drained his glass—
an act so lurid, so voluptuous,
we felt we had to turn away, though Pete,
our Mexican maitre'd whose real name
was Pedro, cut him off at three—no more.
The other two were measured out at five
and six PM, exactly one each hour
like medication in a hospital.
At first I thought him crazy, just a bum
with nowhere else to go, a holdover
from the big bands blasting from my father's
78s. But the clientele loved him,
and the ladies liked his patter when he
wasn't' drunk, flattering them with unctuous

jokes, and leering coyly at the kids.
"Hey, Charlie, you've got your head up your past!"
someone shouted once, and Charlie
slammed his fist on the organ, then glared
at the room: "Who said that!" he thundered,
"And what do you know about music?
I oughta leave." But Charlie stayed, because
humiliation is only a step from pride
and failure has no fixed address.
I even grew to like him and his music—
he was part of summer. Without him
something might be missing, a treasured part
of the past, a piece of ourselves, floating off
unnoticed to be swallowed in the haze
at mid-lake where boats would drift, and vanish.

HIGH DIVER

Straight-backed, clean-limbed, freckled like a trout
she stands at the edge of the high board
defiant and ashamed at once, conscious
of our eyes on her, this diver all of seventeen
whose body is a beauty she can barely comprehend.

The boys shout insults, shove each other
in their awkwardness, half awed that she would step out
on the trembling board to risk our gaze
and the water's bright enticement, smooth but hard
beneath her. Their catcalls echo off the walls.

I cannot tell you how she looks, poised on the cusp
of adolescence, this girl fading into the woman
she'll become, sylph-like in her tight suit,
hair a frazzled halo, arms held up like a sleepwalker
trying to contain herself and blot out their cries.

Now she pivots like a dancer, gripping the board
with her toes, and rises as it quivers with her weight
then settles again. She waits until it stops,
until she gathers herself up to balance there,
tall and undeniable, her back to us in the withering light.

Suddenly her knees bend, spring up, and bend once more,
then toss her up and out into the shocked air
where she clasps her knees between her arms
like a fetus rolling backward in a perfect arc,
then lets them go again and straightens in a long fall.

And then her fingers tear the water open and her body
disappears into the pool, nothing but a splash
to mark where she once was, and the boys turn
to one another, hushed, feeling their own bodies
falling perilously through childhood, past mockery into love.

STAG FILM

"Poontang!," someone yelped, but I thought *beautiful*.
A dozen of us huddled in the dark
to jeer a woman luminescent as a ghost.
Our faces flickered in a shaft of light
the rickety projector branded on a wall.
We sat faithfully through each position
poised for the thrill of a final cum shot.

Each new angle drew a catcall from us
sparking hoots of adolescent laughter
that masked our nervousness. But no one left
or even budged from where we sat transfixed.
I mocked her with the rest, but secretly
feasted on her body, her flesh, her lips,
and each nipple, luscious as a cumquat.

FAMILY FACTORY

There were two employees: myself and Jurgis,
a Lithuanian who hardly spoke—in English,
or anything else—the words sealed up in him
like the concrete mix we bagged all summer,

a blend the owner had invented, and built
his own factory to produce. *What-a-Crete,*
he called it, "Just add water" in the right amount
and it would "set forever, like steel."

Above the roof, a huge hopper with a funnel
that fed a nozzle in the room below
so *What-a-Crete* would come sloughing down
in a rush of powder, gravel, and dirt,

each rush a measured amount to fill the bags
that rolled beneath the nozzle, one
by one, on a short conveyer belt. My job
was simple: grasp each bag by the top

and fold it over, run it through a sewing
machine that stitched it shut, and heave the bag
onto a waiting pallet on the floor. We wore
white paper masks to filter the dust,

so we looked like physicians: "Surgeons of sand
and gravel," I joked, but Jurgis never smiled
and the owner sat inside his office
grimacing at old accounts. When we'd fill

a pallet, I would drive the fork lift up,
slip the tongs between the slats, and raise
it high, then swivel to replace it once again
among the others in the factory aisles.

Sometimes I'd miss and puncture the bags
with a tong, which brought the owner
out, waving his cane in the air like a saber.
Watch what you're doing! and I'd apologize

then take my place again on the line.
But Jurgis never yelled. He'd lost everyone:
parents, friends, his younger brother
Gvidas, whom the Russians tortured until

he spilled it all—names, dates—his perforated body
tossed into an unmarked grave. And here
was Jurgis, exiled with a stupid American boy,
measuring the earth, filling each bag
again tenderly, his heart set, hardened forever.

DRUMMER

Freddie Fisk—that was his name— tall, loose-limbed
and string-bean skinny, whose arms flailed
when he beat time on his traps, a sharp-elbowed hammerer
with a skeletal smile. Freddie owned the hardware store,
having left drumming for turpentine and the price of nails.

He hailed from somewhere in the South— Jersey or New York—
where he drummed for peanuts one night a week
in those seaside haunts that crowd the coast like barnacles
on a rusting boat. In New England he was out of place,
a quick-witted Ichabod with city roots, shifty-eyed and sleek.

My parents made a fuss over Freddie's "real" career,
and I thought Freddie was a star. But looking back,
I see Freddie was a part-time sideman who never got his break,
but drummed up something else: a wife and two kids
as lank and wiry as him. Maybe that was his mistake.

Or maybe he just stood back drop-jawed one night when someone
played so brilliantly it felt like he was beating Freddie
right out of his dreams; some jive-ass jazzman born to rhythm
and the blur of speeding hands and feet. Sometimes
something cures us by defeat and leaves us lesser, but alive.

However it was, Freddie only drummed for us, Sunday evenings
in his cramped apartment there above the batteries and saws.
We'd stand around, goggle-eyed and awed, while Freddie
crashed his cymbals, and we thought, *Freddie's really something!*
And grinned like blazes, and beat our hands together in applause.

FRIENDSHIP

First, we broke in. Then we broke every window
in the place. It was quick work, and we were well suited
for it, being young, and inconsolable, and angry.

Of course, the windows were symbolic, but what
did that matter? They broke as well one way
as another, shattering with an unconditional sound.

And who started it, him or me, made no difference
either. We were equal to the task, our bodies
not separate, but a pair of hands ready for the wrecking.

Then we fled, he to his gloating satisfaction, and I
to mine, though I soon began to understand
how actions cause equal and opposite reactions.

When the police arrived, my parents wondered
how I could have done it, hadn't they raised me
better than this, and wasn't I ashamed of myself now?

I was. Which is what led me to implicate him,
and claim he'd started it. In fact, that he had
done it all, and I'd only stood by watching, aghast.

The cop who took this statement eyed me coldly.
He knew better. And soon I broke down, sobbing,
ready to say anything, ready to tell him then

what I had no words to explain until now,
that betrayal is sometimes the greater part of friendship
and friendship's as fragile as glass, as easy to shatter.

HALE-BOPP

You're gone now, solar vagrant
with a long flagrant tail
that sparkled behind you,
cosmic veil trailing gold dust in its wake.
At first you hung above Boston's
statehouse and The Common,
brighter than an incoming flight.
The city's eyes swung upward
surprised to find you there,
interplanetary stranger heralding
the night. You didn't seem a danger
or some fiery annunciation.
But, good Puritans, we kept an eye
on you, looming above us
from your burning pulpit. And later
as I crossed the Atlantic, half
awake hurtling back through time,
you flared in my window
and I peered out, frantic
to get some sleep. But your effulgence
proved greater than my fatigue.
You only faded as we touched
down, ready for a much deserved
vacation and some legendary French
indulgence. Then from a terrace
in Provence I watched you
dazzle sunset with your phosphorescence,
incandecescent as an earring
on a budding starlet in Cannes.
Around the world we watched you
studding the night sky
with your unaccustomed light.
You drove some of us crazy

who were crazy, blessed others
by your presence, an elegant guest,
Denizen of darkness and unpeopled places.
We won't see your like again.

II

SUPER COLLIDER

Protons and neutrons, once thought to be the smallest
particles of matter, being components of the atom,
which are the smallest objects in nature, can be
broken up into even tinier particles called gluons and quarks.

That much is imaginable. Though it begs the question:
are gluons and quarks made up of tinier particles too,
and those particles, tinier still, tinier and tinier until
we're looking at nothing made of particles made of nothing?

Finding this edge between something and nothing: isn't it
like trying to stay awake and fall asleep at the same time
the way you did as a kid, hoping to discover the exact moment
you fell asleep, to experience it as a moment, and not some

vague, overlapping state in which you are neither awake
nor asleep, but both, and unaware, impossible to remember
afterwards, begging a further question: are there hard lines
between states of consciousness or things in nature?

And if time began a fraction of a fraction of a fraction
of a second after the Big Bang, what existed before that Bang?
Eternity? Or the absence of both eternity and time
so that moment couldn't have been waiting forever to happen?

You might be thinking: what does it matter? There's a tunnel
seventeen miles long, an immense ring of concrete and metal
under the border between Switzerland and France which cost
forty billion dollars to build, so it matters to someone.

When you shatter a proton by smashing it into another
proton going the opposite direction at the speed of light,
the protons explode into their component parts—that is: quarks
and gluons. This forms a particle "soup" which reestablishes

itself by cohering again into protons. But in that collision,
other particles are created and forces unleashed
that haven't existed since time began and that's something,
that's really something, though what it is isn't exactly known.

Take the boson: a particle that gives mass to other particles.
But don't all particles have mass to begin with? Isn't that
the definition of a particle, that it has mass and takes up space
and is tangible and real? What's a particle if it doesn't have mass?

And that isn't all. What about dark matter, or antimatter,
that "extension of the concept of the antiparticle" to all matter,
and the possibility of hidden dimensions of space and time
which might also be revealed when those two protons collide.

Not to mention stranglets, but now that I've mentioned them
it's safe to say that they are hypothetical objects consisting
of *up, down,* and *strange* quarks—three types of quarks that exist
which is strange enough to begin with, if you think about it.

They might be only a few femtometers across, but once
they become large enough to be macroscopic they are called
 "quark stars" or even "strange stars," hypothetically speaking.
A strangelet is a small fragment of strange matter.

It's much more complicated than this, but this is enough
to keep most of us busy for years trying to comprehend exactly
what's going on, though one thing is becoming perfectly
clear: "physicists around the world now have a much greater

power to smash the components of atoms together to learn
about their structure," according to the latest articles, though
smashing things to create things seems counter-intuitive,
while smashing things to learn things seems as natural as the boy

on a beach, far from here, who—having dug up
with his shovel a common clam—examines it and turns it
over in his hand, again and again, finds a rock, then two,
and smashes the clam between them to see what's inside.

It's how we question everything. It's who we are. It's what we do.

GLOBAL WARMING

I've been wanting to write a poem about the icecaps,
wondering how to make myself care. It's so huge, this event, like God,
not really anywhere, yet everywhere at once, so hard to grasp
which is why the newspapers go on clucking about political correctness
while pundits let us know that the latest research indicates
the South Beach diet may not be that effective, or even good for us,
and human cloning may soon be a fact, but is it ethical and should we pursue it?

I remember once in Colorado, after a night of carousing, my friends
and I stumbled through town, arms linked, yelling at the top of our lungs:
"The icecaps are mellllllllllting! The icecaps are mellllllllllting!"
each of us a drunken Paul Revere, though we woke no one up,
not a window blazed in that sleeping village, and the next morning
frost spangled the meadows and blood pounded in our heads
the way people in cheap hotels pummel the walls, demanding quiet.

In my poem birds circle a dead seal on the ice, its blood leaking
out into the snow the way strawberries crushed against linen
spread from thread to thread until the original stain is ten times larger
than when it began and birds wheel above, shrieking, waiting for the body to bloat,
then burst, its hidden delicacies exposed until the bones,
clean and ribbed as ice, blend into the snowpack.

In a poem by Lars Gustafsson, a large dog bolts out onto a frozen sea
as his master lags behind, watching the dog rocket into the glare,
running so hard he seems to shimmer as he begins to shrink with the distance,
then vanishes finally into the ripple of light at the edge of the horizon
while the man stands there, calling and calling for the dog to come back.

But he doesn't. Not in Gustafsson's poem anyway. Not even in this one
where I've begun to think about the fact that the human brain shrinks an ounce
every decade after fifty, which means I've lost an ounce so far, an ounce
of memory and time, which doesn't seem so bad, considering how much time we have,
yet I feel like that island in the South Pacific, the small one where fifty people lived
but now it's gone, vanished under rising seas as if it never existed.

Every day, huge hunks split off and plunge into the sea, which has been filmed,
you can watch it on Discovery Channel between promos for "Living Predators
of the African Veldt" and "The Golden Treasures of Tutankhamen."
It's like watching the demolition of an enormous building
which will have catastrophic consequences for every creature on earth,
including micro-life—nits, mites, diatoms, bacilli—the chemical structure
of their tiny world shifting in a cataclysm of infinite degrees
but just enough to swathe them in a genocidal broth of heat and saline.

Still, the pretty young newswoman smiles as she assays the weather map:
"This has been the warmest winter on record," she purrs, making it sound
so reassuring, so fortunate. "Savor these days," she says, and laughs.
Such a gorgeous messenger—no demon or witch, no Sybil—
not even some awe-inspiring angel descending in a blast of light
to make its announcement.

                    But it's worse than nuclear war,
it's irreversible and planetary which is why the peak of Kilimanjaro is now mud,
and Venice takes another stride into the sea. Such a beautiful catastrophe, tipping towards
Eden, then farther, into the desert which in a hundred years will be almost everywhere
and whoever's left will be living at the poles about to vanish into light at the edge
of the horizon. Unfortunate explorers. Savor these incomparable days.

WORLD WIDE WEB

It's a little like Gulliver, pinned down by Liliputians—
the whole planet woven back and forth with invisible bonds of electricity,
the Big Top of everything-there-is staked down in the wind.

But haven't we always been connected, one way or another—
by goat track, torch-wave, smoke signal, arrow-flight?
Hasn't the air been filled with pigeons hauling messages on their legs,
the ocean a blue-maned Pony Express galloping between
distant coasts to deliver its bottle-stoppered notes?
And what about the Pony Express, the real one, intrepid cowboys
streaking deserts, clattering mountains, fording rivers
so fast those ponies soon transmogrified into speeding trucks?

And while we're at it, what of rivers? Weren't they a kind of wire,
connecting Red Wing with New Orleans, Rybinsk and Astrakhan,
watery cables shunting messages across tracts of land
so vast it must have seemed "world-wide" to men with poles
in open boats bearing dispatches from the throne.

Driving the interstate highway system, one thinks of how it weaves
the whole country together in a kind of asphalt net—
the cracked pavement in front of my door in New York
directly linked to the sun-baked tar in front of yours in L. A.

On one of those highways my friend said: "We have the greatest
technologies now to communicate with each other, but almost nothing
to say!" Or like that sign I saw on a building once: "So little to say,
and so much time." But now we have the "World Wide Web,"
sizzling shroud of Ohms bearing messages at warp speed
between continents and coasts. Words without substance,
a language, at last, of pure light spoken by machines that think
in streams of digits and pixels, that Pointillism of hyperspace
painting a picture of universal communication and understanding.

Yet what is that to the brain, one hundred billion neurons
firing wildly at once, more plentiful than stars, this burning bush
of a human brain from which voices emanate as from a sacred cave?
And what is that to a strand of DNA—microcosmic braid of species,
boundless helix of generations, myriad-skein of eternal life?

Network, system, web, mesh, maze, tapestry, reticulum, grid.

What rage for connection! What urge to unite! To be less
than single, more than one, unconcerned finally
with what is communicated, but communion itself.
This need to reach out, to bridge the gap, to obliterate
the distance between other and self.
This world-wide desire to be contacted and found.

FOREST

No undergrowth   and the trees widely spaced   so to walk
in the forest is like walking through a public building

at least   one kind of forest   but there is another

empire of moss   kingdom of cambium and phloem

———————————

If the mind is known   a sunblown clearing in the trees
more is hidden   or is the mind itself a forest

an abstract tangle   clogged with shattered stumps and thorns

———————————

Heading up the mountain   I was less than Hansel
and more a swaggering naif   the only darkness

what the trees might scatter   stippling the path

dawn extruded dowels and golden planes of light   fans
of luminescence   thick with motes

———————————

Is it possible
to walk in one forest   without walking in the other

here and there   spines of boulders knuckle up
a stump narrates its memory of flame and drought

———————————

Trees are singular   yet can't be seen   only the woods
massing their fabric of leaves   only the fabric's tearing
and repair   the water's soft thread

———————————

I'm looking for a door
that will allow me to enter the forest

leafmeal   pine duff   scurf of seasons

I know what I'm looking for   but I don't know where it is
or maybe I know where it is

but I don't know what I'm looking for

———————————

To clear the forest will do no good

for what is left is its absence   and so the forest
re-asserts itself   its remembered paths

and coverts   thickets of memory in which we lose ourselves

———————————

A single trunk might bring it back   or a leaf
sunlight   too   is a wilderness   woven into green spires

———————————

Whatever we have neglected or haven't done
that is the forest   so the woods are a kind of time   a clock
whose hands are foliage and rain   or is the forest
a cemetery   an overloaded ship   a smoky den

———————————

Whatever it is or resembles   it's everywhere   like
a boy who leaves home to find out he's become someone else
a boy whose footsteps   whose memories   are bread

———————————

Leaving the forest   we carry it with us
a spreading umbrage   growing vaster with years

it breaks   finally   out of us   overrunning the pales
the gardens   the manicured lawns   until

the edge of one forest touches the other   and that's
where it finally ends   and the real forest begins

THE HIEROPHANT OF HARTFORD

For Wallace Stevens

I.

Never has a noble vocabulary been loved so much:

Bronze, first, and then *procession,* in all its forms,
As in: "The bronze processional of the oaks…"

Genius, linked with many nouns, as though the world
Were sentient, a student of experience and time.

Then *summer,* always, that genial season
With its carnivorous clouds and inestimable flowers.

He loved the *sun*'s fiery accompaniment and pagan light;
The sea gnashing its immense and aqueous teeth.

And he loved to say words more than once,
As in "The sun's bronze genius above the summer sea."

II.

A world needs trees to jungle it, and storied beasts.

The mind's occult menagerie was his:
A polychrome of swans and peacocks, owls and doves.

Golden-eyed macaws made music in the boughs
While cinnamon trees sweetened evening's purple fall.

All this tangled in the mind's vast hinterland
As summer's genius greened the season's blue pavilion.

And in that Paradise of Adams, Badroulbadour appeared,
Gaunt Fernando, silly Crispin and sad Ramon,

Silent interlocutors whose sisters sang as well
Faceless as the sea-bronzed sand where the wind stirred.

III.

The objective world and the mind are separate, but one.

On points of paradox his poems danced.
Such was his conundrum to puzzle in exact verses.

Master of the pure word, sesquipedalia of the sentence,
Palm and hemlock were the efflorescence of his thought,

Feral sea and river his watery amanuenses,
Or he was theirs. Order was an idea posed in equipoise.

Yet the world is empty of our spirit, as we of its,
If spirit it has, known only of Imagination's avatar.

No prayer but the snowman's numb avowels.
No gods but satyrs under the sun's broad bacchanal.

IV.

He was the singer of the intellect's baroque enchantments.

On ordinary evenings he might pause to scry the heavens
Or the solemn houses of Connecticut,

The clapboard sameness of bourgeois habitations
In which inmates, gowned like ghosts, serenely roamed.

Cicisbeo of Hartford's plain allurements,
A fictive music played across the movement of his lines,

Orchestrations of the greater Vocalissimus
That trembled solely on the spirit with a soundless sound.

O prodigal, soloist of the mind's Reality, the scrawny cry—
The poem's elemental *it*, whatever it its it is.

A THOUSAND KIM

"Dutch Schultz's deathbed ravings covered a wide range—all the way
      from mysterious million-dollar deals to assorted pals
          and double-XX guys to Communists, of all things.
     One sentence confounded everybody, even
the poets: *A boy has never wept, nor dashed a thousand kim.*
      What did the dying badman mean?" Well, who knows.
        History may never repeat itself, but it stutters.
     Time machineguns events at us, and we stagger,
bleeding from the holes in our hearts. On television
     a veteran back from Iraq boasts "I looked death in the eye.
       I fought with death and I won." He glares
    at the camera, minus two legs (below the knee), the left side
       of his face disfigured, a ruddy lump of scars.
"How many people can say that?" he asks. No one replies. His image
     fades, and a commercial for Ambien splashes onto the screen.

§

It's hard to rest these days. Nightmares gallop through our brains,
     lids jitter in REM sleep, even our legs lurch and need
       to be calmed. *Suffering and death are of little interest
to the artist,* thought Gertrude Stein and as the Second
World War approached, remarked: "I could not see why there being
    so many more of them made it any more interesting."
     Well who knows. A hundred kim, or a thousand
    are hard to visualize. That's why the government hides the bodies
and lead still kills, leaching into the brain from the brightly painted surfaces
    of toys. "No world," said my friend, "could be stranger
     than this one!" and I was beginning to see what he meant.

§

What a poor tool our brains are for making sense of anything.
        From the *Falx cerebri* down to the *Teritorium of Cerebellum,*
                we're stymied, and a bullet doesn't help, or a fleck
        of carcinogenic paint lodged neatly in the forebrain. Every time I pass
a child on the corner I think: "He could be packing a gun." Then I laugh
        at my own foolishness. But last night in my sleep a child shot
                another child, and I did nothing. I didn't even wake up
        until a garbage truck slammed down our street and for some reason
I thought of Will Durant, the philosopher, who calculated that there have been
        only twenty-nine years in all of human history during which
                there was not a war underway somewhere.
        Maybe we should wear seatbelts when we go to bed. Maybe
we should ban lead from the body altogether, so we never have to endure
        the sight of a mutilated boy weeping.

§

If young minds soak up knowledge "like a sponge," age wrings
        it all out again until compassion becomes bloodlust and history
                is honed to a single point. Maybe that point,
        smaller than a period, in which the universe was packed
before the Big Bang ripped it open and out sprang St. Francis and Jeffrey
        Dahmer, Ghandi and Dutch Schultz, each animated by a kind
                of brain. "Dinosaurs had two brains," my friend said, "for all
        the good it did them—one in the head, and one in the tail." Scaly
hook-and-ladders negotiating pre-history's curves, though a comet
        did them in, like a stray bullet wandering a neighborhood
                until it found its random target, earth, which some
        have likened to a massive brain with its folded mountains,
its bright ideas like evolution or volcanoes spewing lava into the sea.

§

After World War I the Surrealists wanted to go to sleep forever,
        and poor Apollonaire did, but not before a sliver of the real world
                pierced his skull and a crowd of citizens massed outside
        his window chanting *Guillaume! Guillaume!* like a mother
calling her child home at dusk, while the movies of George Méliès
        were melted down to make heels for soldiers' boots.
                This was no dream, but a bizarre variant of beating
        ploughshares into swords as the French army plodded off to war
shod in Méliés' films, winsome illusions of that inventive movie-house magician.
        Death longs to infiltrate the world and experience life, if only
                briefly, borrowing our bodies before turning back
        into its own emptiness. Just this morning, twelve-feet high on the side
of a bus, the picture of a man grinning warmly, with blood-spattered
        forehead and cheeks, rolled past with the legend:
                "America's favorite serial killer" spelled out in red paint,
        a sentence that might confound anyone, while the rest of us
shopped for artichokes and bagels, cut-rate carpets and white wine.

§

The world offers up its runes, its daily figments of reality, though
        I don't mean to exclude myself in any of this, as no one is excluded,
                but dragged ineluctably into to a wide net
like that purse-seine Robinson Jeffers imagined, all of us victims
        of interdependence until "Now there is no escape. We have gathered
                vast populations incapable of free survival…each person himself
        helpless," and so on. A thousand kim, a million kim. Like this pale
boy swaggering past, in black denim trousers and t-shirt, chrome studs
        glittering in his ears and lips in self-crucifixion, *Fuck You Very Much*
                stenciled across his chest. The world to him is a madhouse,
        a threat to his existence. It's a no-brainer as far as he's
concerned. Wars and future wars: the same war burning from decade
        to decade, as a pile of leaves catches fire from leaf to leaf,

or a forest from tree to tree. The same spark of anger from ten
thousand years ago when Cain picked up that rock and brained his brother.

§

But no one can remember that far back. Memory contains its own
        erasure, each generation another chapter in history's
                long amnesia. When a politician on t.v. says "we're going
        to see that this never happens again" I laugh out loud,
though it gives me no pleasure. I think of all the "eternal flames"
        burning around the world, polished cenotaphs
                containing nothing but the memory of unknown
        soldiers, their limbs so scattered they couldn't gather them up
to give them a decent burial. "History teaches us…" he's now saying,
        the TV announcer, and I wonder what he'll say next?
                If Cain and Dutch Schultz were brothers,
        what can we expect from two pounds of marbled
gray matter Hippocrates first located as the source
        of the mind—though long before that the Greeks and Egyptians
thought the mind resided in the heart, which is far more desirable.

§

Memories are dreams from which we don't wake up, until they become
        so distant it's as if they don't matter at all, or somehow never existed.
                Is hope a recurrent dream from which we never
        wake? The other night my wife half-sat up in bed and said
very clearly, very firmly, "Time promise in paradise everything is well,"
        then fell asleep again, and I did too, hoping that dreams
                still have validity and forecast the future as they did for the Pharoahs
        who ignored them at their peril, or woke in celebration of the coming
harvest, or a daughter's impending wedding. Who knows. But this morning
        in front of me in line at the bank, I stared at a question mark

tattooed on the back of a man's shaved head, there, at the base
of his skull where his spinal cord met his brain, the curled
blue hook of ink floating over a point, no bigger than a period, out of which
the universe might one day emerge, or into which
it might just as suddenly again, and without reason, disappear.

III

TOMORROW AND TOMORROW

Of *course* there's an afterlife, and one
after that, and another, etc., until the afterlives
circle eternity to become the life
you lived before this one, making this one
an afterlife too. No wonder you sleep late,
trying to avoid the little tasks and obligations,
the aches and pains that make up yesterday's afterlife
which is, of course, today's present.
There's no avoiding that. Though your head
aches to think of it, and you'd rather
linger by the window with your coffee
watching the neighbor's dog chase its tail.
Still, you can't help thinking that maybe
the present is just a beach on which all our yesterdays
have washed up, hollow and resounding.
But resounding with what? This will get you
nowhere, you think, and go back
for another cup, though it occurs to you
that you've done this all before too—
not only the cup of coffee you just drank,
but all the coffees on all those other mornings…
Now you're back where you started,
and your head aches again, and you want
nothing but to sit there peacefully in the window
watching the neighbor's dog chase its tail
never really catching it, yet never giving up.

LOVE POEM

Once, my poor distracted wife
put her bra into the freezer, where I found it in the morning
stiff with frost. And once, she put rice
into the bottom of my cup of tea, mistaking it for sugar—
the rice, that is—thinking it would sweeten
the cloudy brown dregs, then handed it to me with a smile.
And once, wearing only her nightgown
and my laced-up hiking boots, she stepped daintily
out into the snow behind our house and waded
through three-foot drifts like a bride lifting the hem of her skirt—
a memory clearer to me than our own wedding.
Sometimes love is not that serious, and what we love
is joy and the love joy brings. Though even that
is too complicated for what I feel when I recall her
standing in her garden in muddy overalls,
hands encased in thick gloves, rubber boots
up to her knees, a trowel or mulching fork in one of her hands.
Because love isn't always formal, either,
decked out in evening gowns, carrying an expensive
handbag and wearing a string of pearls.
Mostly it's frowsy and real, red-faced and smacking
its lips in the morning, a thread of dried blood
where the razor with its one keen tooth bit into a delicate ankle.
Love is there every day, the smell of cooking
in its hair, lips chaffed in the first frost,
argumentative and cross, crying at nothing,
then laughing hysterically at its own joke, or yours
as it trudges through snow or fishes a bra out of the freezer
where it has hibernated overnight. Seriously.

READING THE VICTORIANS

Such bulky phrases, big as sofas, heavy
as carved tables or mahogany desks.
Such husky words: straight from Latin,
polysyllabic and dense, each word a sentence in itself
clutching Europe's history in its roots.
Long periodic thoughts, clause by clause
rattle past like open trolleys hauling
valuable freight, Tiffany insights, Gallé views.
Victorian minds were not like ours.
Their brains had high brick stoops, ornate doors,
winding stairways into candlelit rooms.

All we need's a hot plate and a cozy Futon,
old fruit crates to display our thoughts.
Our sentences are sunny, elemental as unframed prints.
We're not the first to live here
nor the last to toss our store-bought rugs
upon the floor. What we say is trimmed
and packaged, subject to inspection,
uttered in a heartbeat under heavy pressure.
When we raise our voices, the neighbors bang the wall.

FOR MIKLÓS RADNÓTI

You lie awake among the snores and groans,
the stifled cries that nightmares cause,
haunting the sleepers. Outside, fog settles
on the barracks like a blanket on a corpse.

Halfway across the world I'm awake too,
a child only six months old, whose mother
cups his head with a tender hand, to whom
she coos, then tucks him under soft covers.

By what light do you scratch a letter
to your wife—not just a letter but a poem
in which you tell her of your dreams, the dream
of every man there: "Ah, does *our* home

still exist…Is it still as when we left it?"
Perhaps the moon, sliced by sharp wires
spills into the cramped confines of your room,
spreading the hellish glint of pale fires.

Those scratchings in the dark have reached us here
Miklós, in the light of a future age
you never lived to see. And today it's me,
I'm the one who reads your poems, page by page,

and lives your nightmares with you, though
I never had to cower like a trapped
animal. We shared nothing but the fragment
of a year until fate found you and stopped

your words. But I'm alive to tell you
that your poems survive, your poems were saved
and are read, even in this alien tongue,
though you took them with you to your grave.

OLD HOWARD

I saw Howard Nemerov once, strolling
down a path on the C. U. campus. It
was spring and the new-leaved trees were rolling
in the breeze and the birds were singing. But

there he was, a shock of iron-gray hair
above the obligatory tweed vest.
It must have been a reading brought him there.
I can't remember. He seemed distressed,

heavy-footed and obviously sick
lumbering along like a wounded bear.
My friend whispered: *That's Nemerov, quick,*
and pointed straightway where I looked. *Don't stare!*

I was a not-so-young grad student who'd
returned to school after years of working
in the "real world" where I'd learned that work could
dry up your soul, though I wasn't shirking

my obligations—only trying to find
them again and shift my priorities.
Seeing Nemerov might have changed my mind,
shuffling along there under the trees.

He'd spent a lifetime trying to reconcile
his displeasure in poems few understood.
I think he died soon after of sheer bile,
too damned intelligent for his own good.

MEETING BLY FOR THE FIRST TIME THE THIRD TIME

When I meet Robert Bly, his eyes drift into a middle
distance over my shoulder, then even farther, to a place
where "distance" no longer exists. I become transparent
as an alabaster death mask. Medieval philosophers brush me aside,
Scotus and Aquinas with their mortar boards and gowns,
Erasmus, his sour Dutch face ravaged by the plague of knowledge.
Fabulous beasts leap from the friezes of ancient Ur
to parade along the streets of Minneapolis and St. Paul,
sphinx and hippogriff, basilisk and chimera,
their stone wings brushing the edges of Starbucks and The Gap.
I might be meeting an angel, the vast white halo of his hair,
the washed-out blue of his eyes which register a depth
that cannot be plumbed, or a boredom so heavy
his soul has fled and converses now with someone
in another city, while his hand still rests in mine,
the empty husk of something that has become something else.
He speaks like a flute, and says each word twice.
I stand in a desert, saying over and over again, my name.

MELVILLE AT THE CUSTOM HOUSE

Every ship whose bow nudged this island
cursed you, cargoed with its distance,
exotic lands from which you once drew plots.
Those first two novels baited fame.
But no longer. Without your public
you were exiled sure as any outcast on his rock,
and that building was a rock, a headland
of indifference carved in marble.
The toll was severe. Drinking, rages, the critics'
savagery greater than any you had known.
Your wife screeched stories of abuse,
your children drifted off to separate deaths.
You trained weak eyes on pages wrought
with numbers enigmatic as Queequeg's tattoos.
Six days a week for nineteen years,
four bucks a day. It adds up. Back home at night,
you squinted at the lines of *Clarel,* that pilgrimage
in verse. God remained a phantom sail
on a lost horizon, something you could not believe
nor stop pursuing. At dawn, without fail,
you'd re-embark down Broadway towards the office
circled by the screams of brokers picking
at the carcass of the Stock Exchange.
You died in your own room, loved only
by Elizabeth, a few grandchildren disposed
around the bed. Never mind that stone
at Woodlawn with its empty scroll
far from Manhattan and the Custom House.
      That building was your tomb.

TO A FRIEND IN HIS ILLNESS

I think of you sitting in the frail light
of a far coast, summer over, autumn
about to begin—chill dawns, longer nights,
the last warm breeze shuffling the poplars.
Evening arrives, like some early guest.
And there you are, half asleep on the terrace,
a half-read book half-open on your chest.

Who knows when illness starts? At first, we're fine.
The body hides its secret, like a thing
conceived—a cluster of errant cells line
up to form their own enterprise, then cling
together and begin to grow. Before
we know it, we are not ourselves, and then
we know it, and the common lives we bore
begin to take on new complexities.

Our ways change. We chart the course of disease
the way explorers consult strange stars,
heading inevitably towards the unknown.
But what's the pronoun "we" to you? A word
that you could do without. You're there alone,
watching the body of a hummingbird
hurtle like a spark across the lawn.

Somewhere, a neighbor's dog barks at shadows
and a door slams, shutting out the night.
You could die now as distant windows
flash, one by one, across the darkened land.
Now you close your book, and gaze out
at the poplars' thickening silhouette.
Someday, maybe, if things don't go as planned.

But not this evening. Not just now. Not yet.

A MOMENT

I keep returning to that moment, one
day at your kitchen table with the sun
slanting in through the glass above your sink.
You stood before me, brushing your long hair,
stroke after stroke in the astonished air
while you talked of nothing, and I sipped my drink.

Then suddenly you bent your head, and threw
your hair forward in a bright fan to show
your beauty in a simple act, at once
casual and contrived, while I sat there
like some stone figure in a stone chair—
such blatant beauty required a response.

But I did nothing, though my heart halted
in my chest, a small, numb, exalted
animal, until you tossed that golden wrack
of hair to settle once again upon
your shoulders and you smiled your wan
smile and I recalled myself, and smiled back.

INSIDE JOB

We begin inside until we are outside
which is the other side of the story
though we never forget that inside the beginning
is the ending even if we cannot see it
and inside the ending is the lost beginning,
the yin and yang of everything there is
balanced on the fulcrum of our choice
and inside choice is fate, while inside fate
is a road, long as your life, which choice
has imagined and fate will build
paving over the other choices we might have made
until it may seem that they never existed,
residual possibilities of a fossil life
which remains inside us the way the imprint
of an ancient fern remains inside the mud
that once enclosed it baked into stone
by the early sun that spun wildly in the sky

MURDER ON AVENUE X

is a good title for a novel or a poem, like this one
in which the body of a celebrated showgirl
is found abandoned just outside the precincts
of Coney Island one day in early September
before summer has all but folded its aluminum
beach chair and trudged off through old food wrappers,
plastic beer cups and discarded French fries
which seagulls wrangle from each other like jackals,
screaming and beating their wings.
The body of the dead girl remains undiscovered
in the first few lines of the poem, just a detail in the landscape
which includes the motionless ferris wheel,
the red steel tower for heart-stopping parachute drops,
scuffed bumper cars, even the last leathery
diehards scouring the boardwalk for another day
of sunlight scattering over the water as the sun itself
circles lower and lower on the horizon
and far ships seem to hurry away, like distant stars.
Everything flees the scene, the body, the police,
who haven't arrived yet, who haven't even
been informed, because the dead girl
is still lying there, undetected, ready to emerge
as the secret meaning of this poem, its hidden subject,
the gorgeous young dancer giving up her life for art.
Meanwhile, trains pass every ten minutes,
but no one notices anything unusual, anything
out of the ordinary, no one knows a thing about the men
at the end of the pier who toss bloody fish heads
into the water to attract crabs, and pull up flat,
silvery fish no bigger than saucers—
the culprit, the real one, slips through our fingers,
eludes all attempts at capture, can't even

be identified, any more than the meaning of this poem,
only glimpsed partially, here and there—
possibly the man in the line-up with the gold tooth,
or the bald one with the blurred tattoo,
who knows, maybe even the young punk chewing
gum and glowering at us through the glass—
there's no hard evidence, nothing
conclusive we could put our finger on
only a murder on Avenue X, with no motive, really,
little to go on, and no one to blame.

NEAR ANTWERP

At Mortsel-Oude God station
the round white face of a clock
declares the hour. Its second hand
revolves as though searching
for something, like the sweeping beam
on a radar screen. The trees
must think it's some kind of strange
mollusk winding its way slowly,
infinitely slowly, back into itself,
spiral by spiral through a narrowing
set of rooms. There are no people
around. Nothing has happened
since 1943. The trees turn
toward each other, silent and appraising.
Death still squats over Belgium,
a blank sky herding umbrellas
into the street, interminable rain.
When history returns, it'll be more of the same:
negotiations, betrayal, murder.
Why pay any attention at all
whisper the trees. They turn
their backs, they can't be bothered.

FOR A WOMAN IN PERE LACHAISE

She's the only one who seems to know what's happening.
Otherwise, this group sculpture here at Monument aux Morts—

a number of bone-worn bodies marching towards death,
that door in the middle of a tomb into which some have already stepped—

would seem predictable, corny. The one I love is above me, on the far right
as I stand in front of the monument, a little dizzy in the August heat.

She's half sitting, or squatting, one knee up, one down,
like a girl at a picnic, but her upper body is torqued backwards,

her right arm flung across her breast, left arm raised, elbow cocked,
fingers to her lips blowing a final kiss as she gazes back at all she is leaving behind.

Hard to tell if she's beautiful. Time has eaten her features, scraped them down
to abstract jawbone and nose. Her beauty is in her posture, the way

her right hand touches her breast in disbelief, as if to catch her breath
that wants escape, wants to shape itself into a sudden scream. Her pathos

is in that left hand, fingertips to lips, dismayed at what she knows, just
now, for the fist time, the terrible realization of what is happening,

about which she can do nothing, bound with the others, drawn forward
despite her retrospective gaze. It is her helplessness that appeals,

her brokenness, torn between worlds, love and regret
carved out of the same stone. Yet she leans towards that looming door

as if something in her body has already acquiesced, something
that knows before she does, and thoughtlessly obeys. Her whole self,

facing two directions, until she isn't there, or anywhere, but there still
for an instant, poised on the last fraction of time she will ever know.

AT THE BLUE GATES

Hendry's Beach, Santa Barbara

Vast   centerless   its frilled borders
beating land   salt-laver and seal pasture
what nightmare forged the lobster's face   the spectral
man-o-war floating in its poisons   wellspring of fishes
the spiked and many-armed   mussel   dogfish   mackerel   skate
endless cycles wheeling like gulls   and out crawls
the walrus   the horseshoe crab   lulled in its pelagic dance
what horrors   what chasms where the light dies
sunken forests   mountains   world-girdler   once-God
drop of dew from time's beginning   drying
on a spiraled arm of stars   we stand and look out   homesick
appalled   here at the blue gates   the land's unraveling end

SOME LATE ADVENTURES WITH THE SOUL

I.

Some days, like today, my soul feels as young as an infant
taking its first sip of milk. The sky looks out from the photograph
of a sky framed on a wall in a room where people walk,
staring into the image of a sky. Outside, of course, the real sky
at which no one is looking for the moment. Across it,
the shadow of something running, as if the earth were burning,
casting an image upwards, and not the other way around.
Maybe it was the sun, wanting only to look up at itself,
wanting to see its own majesty for once, inconceivable, and at a distance.

II.

Clouds hide their ashen faces, and the river lurches between banks
describing its passage south in a blade of sunlight where whole forests
flourish, and die. Far away, under mountains, horses thrust their heads
into that moment of green fire and crickets sing *omni
gloriosa omni* blessing the dust, the wild fractures in the earth.
If I have a soul, it doesn't belong in a church, any more than the forest
which hesitates, each leaf cocked, listening. A man has come out
into his backyard to sit in his lawn chair, and look up,
the pith of his brain greater than anything he can see, and everything beyond.

ACKNOWLEDGEMENTS

Many thanks to the editors of the magazines, in which the following poems appeared, often in slightly different versions:

"Melville at the Custom House" was first published in *River Oak Review*

"Reading the Victorians" first appeared in *Westbranch*

"At the Summer Lake Club" was first published in *Nightsun*

"Global Warming" first appeared in *Court Green*

"Some Late Adventures with the Soul" appeared in the online journal *Limp Wrist*

"The Hierophant of Hartford" in *Redivider* and later in *Visiting Wallace: Poems Inspired by the Life and Work of Wallace Stevens* (University of Iowa Press, 2009).

"Beyond Babylon" and "Dance Lessons" appeared in *The Same*

"Family Factory" appeared first in *Provincetown Arts*

"High Diver" first appeared in *Water-Stone Review*

"Super Collider" was first published in *The Cortland Review* (online)

"A Thousand Kim" first appeared in *Mudlark* (online)

"World Wide Web" was first published in *Solstice* (online)

"For a Woman at Père Lachaise," and "Near Antwerp" first appeared in *Cerise Press* (online)

"That Street," "Practice," "The Catch," "Drummer," and "Friendship" were first published by *Connotation Press* (online)

"A Moment" first appeared in *Serving House* (online)

"About Time" was published in the anthology, *Because You Asked: Fifteen Years of Questions & Answers with Writers who've Visited Walla Walla,* Edited by Katrina Roberts

"Murder on Avenue X" is for Kristien Hemmerechts

"Time" and "Love Poem" are for my wife, Laure-Anne Bosselaar

"A Moment" is for Marie Ouhrabka

"Melville at the Custom House," and "Stag Film" are for Stephen Dunn

"To a Friend in His Illness" is for Peter Sears

"Tomorrow and Tomorrow" is for Steve Huff

"For Miklós Radnóti" is for Virginia Slachman

The quoted material at the beginning of "A Thousand Kim", including Dutch Schulz's remark, are taken from a book about the early part of the 20th century in America. I have since lost the book in a number of geographical moves, and do not recall the title or the publisher.

Special thanks to Stephen Dunn, Virginia Slachman, Philip Dacey, Thom Ward, Steve Huff, Philip Memmer and Laure-Anne Bosselaar, who helped greatly with these poems.

ABOUT THE AUTHOR

Kurt Brown founded the Aspen Writers' Conference, and Writers' Conferences & Centers. He is the author of six chapbooks and six full-length collections of poetry. He is currently an editor for the online journal *MEAD: The Magazine of Literature and Libations* and has edited ten anthologies of poetry, including his newest (with Harold Schechter) *Killer Verse: Poems about Murder and Mayhem.* His memoir, *LOST SHEEP: Aspen's Counterculture in the 1970s,* was published by Conundrum Press in 2012. He taught for many years at Sarah Lawrence College in New York and now lives in Santa Barbara, California.